Experiences of Adolescents Living with Type 1 Diabetes Mellitus whilst Negotiating with the Society

Gloria Tshabalala

Submitted as part of the MSc degree in diabetes
University of Surrey, Roehampton, 2003

ISBN 978-1-956001-21-1 (paperback)
ISBN 978-1-956001-22-8 (eBook)

Copyright © 2021 by Gloria Tshabalala

All rights reserved. No part of this publication may be reproduced, distributed, or transmitted in any form or by any means, including photocopying, recording, or other electronic or mechanical methods without the prior written permission of the publisher.

Printed in the United States of America

Dedication

This book is dedicated to my late parents, Emma and Chambers Nkabinde who showed me love, patience, and resilience during hard times.

Acknowledgements

I have learned that writing a book is not an easy task because it needs a support system. I would therefore like to express my sincerest gratitude to all those who supported me.

My Publisher, AuthorHouse for supporting me in every step especially Dorothy Lee who tirelessly gave me guidance using electronic media.

My children Nhlanhla, Lindiwe, and Bongiwe for their encouragement and support. Bongiwe also helped with typing the script.

Professor Geoff Gill, a Consultant Physician in Diabetes, Endocrinology, and General Medicine who guided and supported me in the early 1990s to publish papers on diabetes journals.

My colleague, Ines Oliveira who proofread the script and helped me to send it electronically to the Publisher.

I would like also like to thank The Hillingdon Hospital NHS Foundation Trust and Diabeticare for allowing me to conduct the study.

I am very grateful to all the adolescents and their parents who allowed me to question them and for their genuine answers.

Many thanks to all those who guided and supported me during my personal and professional development.

Abstract

This qualitative study aims to explore the experiences of adolescents living with type 1 diabetes mellitus (TIDM). This is a chronic condition characterised by abnormally high blood glucose brought on by lack of insulin, and it is treated with insulin injections as there is no medical cure. More specifically, the study examines how the sufferer manages the illness and copes with the perception of stigmatisation which is related to this condition. Despite the existence of research into living and coping with some chronic conditions, research on TIDM, particularly with the use of qualitative methodologies, is limited. A review of the literature indicates that research on the stigma associated with chronic illnesses, particularly those which are functional and invisible (i.e. in which the symptoms are not externally visible), is insufficient.

In-depth interviews were conducted with nine volunteers (five females and four males) who were aged between sixteen and nineteen years and had a diagnosis of TIDM for a minimum of two years. An analysis of the interviews was based on a grounded theory methodology whereby a number of categories were generated. From these, two core categories emerged: assimilation/accommodation and stigmatisation. These represent sufferers' attempt to cope with the experience of TIDM and manage perceived stigmas associated with the unacceptability of the symptoms and invalidation (caused by lack of sympathy or belief by others as there are no physical abnormalities) of their condition.

Parts of the implications of these findings indicate that a departure from the medical model to one of management with consideration of psychosocial issues is important in facilitating sufferers' adjustment to the chronic condition. Suggestions for further qualitative research into TIDM and other invisible chronic illnesses are presented along with the limitations and transferability of this research.

Contents

1. Introduction 1
   1.1 Disease versus illness..1
   1.2 Chronic illness 2
   1.2.1 The concept of chronic illness 3
   1.2.2 Methodology issues in chronic illness research...........5
   1.2.3 Responses to chronic illness................................5
   1.3 Social identity and self-concept in chronic illness 6
   1.3.1 Identity control in chronic illness 8
   1.4 The experience of stigma in chronic illness...............8
   1.4.1 Information disclosure....................................10
   1.5 Coping with chronic illness 11
   1.5.1 Coping through control 13
   1.6 TIDM as a chronic illness..14
   1.6.1 TIDM as a chronic disorder 15
   1.6.2 The invisibility of TIDM...................................16
   1.6.3 The causes and management of TIDM...........16
   1.7 The experience of stigma in TIDM 17
   1.8 Methodological issues in TIDM research.................18
   1.9 Focus of current research 18
   1.9.1 Research aims...19
   1.9.2 Rationale..20
2. Method..21
   2.1 The qualitative approach 21
   2.1.1 Rationale for using qualitative method 22
   2.2 Grounded theory..23
   2.2.1 Grounded theory revised 24

  2.3 Ethical issues 25
  2.3.1 Ethical approval..26
  2.3.2 Anonymity and confidentiality..........................26
  2.4 Design..27
  2.4.1 Sampling...27
  2.4.2 Criteria for participation 28
  2.4.3 Adolescents excluded from the study 29
  2.4.4 Participants 29
  2.4.5 Instruments..30
  2.5 Qualitative data collection and analysis 31
  2.5.1 Data collection 31
  2.5.2 Data analysis 32
  2.5.2.1 Line-by-line coding..32
  2.5.2.2 Focused coding...33
  2.5.2.3 Selective coding..34
  2.5.2.4 Memo writing 34
3. Results 35
  3.1 Demography of participants..................................35
  3.2 Interview extracts 36
4. Discussion..41
  4.1 Self-identity..42
  4.2 Experiences of living with T1DM 43
  4.3 Stigma from health professionals 45
  4.4 Social stigma 46
  4.5 Validity of the study 47
  4.5.1 Sensemaking/understanding...............................48
  4.5.2 Strategies to control symptoms..........................48
  4.5.3 Self-identity change...49
  4.5.4 Invalidation/lack of belief...................................49
  4.5.5 Social unacceptability of T1DM 50
  4.5.6 Strategies of appearing normal...........................50
  4.6 Reliability of the instrument..................................51
5. Conclusion 53
6. Implications of the study..56
7. Limitations of the study...57
8. Recommendations 58
9. References..59

1

Introduction

The present study explored the experiences of adolescents living with type 1 diabetes mellitus (TIDM). This condition has been described as abnormally high blood glucose caused by a lack of insulin in the body and is experienced by the sufferer as a chronic illness. The purpose of the research was to broaden the current understanding of how this illness might affect the individual psychosocially, particularly in terms of coping with perceived stigma.

The study is introduced by a summary of the literature on chronic illness and the experiences of living with chronic illness. This is followed by consideration of the specific effects of the experience of stigma and coping with chronic illness. TIDM will be introduced with a discussion of issues surrounding the diagnosis of TIDM, the label of a functional disorder, the invisibility of the illness, psychosocial factors, stigma, and gender roles. Finally, the rationale for this study and the specific focus of the enquiry is proposed.

1.1 Disease versus illness

Conrad (1987) believes it is important to distinguish between disease and illness. Disease can be conceptualised as an abnormal physiological state or process, whereas illness can be understood as psychosocial phenomena such as behavioural changes, personal subjective experience, and perceptions occurring within a social context that may accompany a physiological process. However, disease is not necessarily a prerequisite of illness since the individual may experience illness without disease, that is have symptoms with no abnormal organic cause. This is applicable to the diagnosis of TIDM where there is no discernible disease, but the individual continues to experience unpleasant physical symptoms. In accordance with this definition, TIDM will be referred to as an illness or condition within this text.

1.2 Chronic illness

TIDM has been deemed a chronic condition given the enduring nature of the illness and lack of cure. The term *chronic illness* has been applied to several disorders that involve impairment of bodily function over a prolonged period of time (Abram et al., 1980). Lawrence (1994) noted that during the twentieth century the new scientific approaches to disease and illness were associated with social and sometimes political reform. By 1920 in Europe and North America, the idea of disease as individual pathology had become the dominant paradigm and was inextricably linked to the development of a bounded medical profession exerting almost complete jurisdiction over illness and its treatment. This has an impact on individuals who are expected to manage the chronic condition and also cope with the perceived stigma.

This has implications for the healthcare system, as infectious and acute diseases, to which the medical system has been tailored, have decreased because of improvements in healthcare and treatment options. In contrast to the time-limited nature of acute illness, chronic conditions are characterised by the necessity of lifelong management, often without the hope of medical cure (Kelleher, 1988).

INTRODUCTION

Furthermore, healthcare services require that the individual be responsible for living and coping with chronic illness and its psychosocial consequences. Such expectations highlight the inadequacy of the medical model in promoting adaptation to chronic illness.

1.2.1 The concept of chronic illness

First, the 'outsider perspective' (Conrad, 1987) views illness and the sufferer as an object from within a Western medical framework. Within the medical model, the body is viewed as a mechanical physiological system, and illness is defined in terms of objective physical systems which are separate from the mind (Radley, 1997). However, the inadequacy of this model in considering psychosocial issues and how the individual copes with chronic illness has warranted an alternative conceptualisation. To account for both biological and social facets of illness, Kelly and Field (1996) suggested that illness should be constructed as a 'multi-phenomenal experience'. That is, illness does not exist purely on a physical, biological level but is integrated with psychological and social phenomena.

Second, the 'insider perspective' (Conrad, 1987), representing the theoretical approach of this study, focuses on the subjective experience of living with illness, that is how the illness is negotiated and managed in everyday life experience. This more comprehensive approach not only considers physical processes but also incorporates how the individual makes sense of, responds to, copes with, and adapts to the illness (Kleinman, 1988). Hence the mind and body are regarded as integrated. It was noted by Strauss (1975) that there was a growing impact of degenerative and chronic illness and that the related predominance of chronic physical and psychosomatic illness needed management and care to supersede treatment and cure (Gerhardt, 1989).

Whilst acknowledging that the concept of illness is socially informed, initial enquiries, such as Parsons' sick role theory (Parsons, 1951), which suggest illness is a deviant social role, continued to examine illness within the medical contexts (Idler, 1979). The emphasis on objective human social reality and illness role behaviours did not recognise the subjective social reality, that is the meaning that individuals give to the situation of illness. In stating that 'we not only have bodies, but we are bodies', Idler was implying that the continuity of not only the self and the body but also of the individual's world of illness exists within the context of the larger world.

It is appreciated that although each individual's experience of chronic illness is unique, a number of common themes have emerged from the literature (Abram, 1980). These include the following:

1) The threat that illness poses to the sufferer's personal integrity, that changing self-identity, which may result in lowered self-esteem.
2) How the illness is coped with, which is determined by how the individual deals with personal meanings attributed to the illness resulting in either adjustment or maladjustment.
3) The impact of illness on the person's lifestyle and interpersonal relation often requiring many changes and restrictions such as types of food to avoided or eaten in moderation and jobs offered.

Physicians and society may not understand how the individual will feel and adapt to the illness. They may not show support and sympathy expected by the individual living with chronic illness.

INTRODUCTION

1.2.2 Methodology issues in chronic illness research

When the concept of chronic illness shifted from the medical model to a more holistic biopsychosocial approach, methodological approaches were also required to change. Quantitative approaches, with the emphasis on objectivity and statistical analysis, complemented the medical model but not the holistic approach. However, Yardley (1997) criticised the proliferation of quantitative research on chronic illness which reinforces the role of the individual as a patient, associated with the medical model. She emphasised that by reinforcing individual experiences as objective measures which can be subjected to statistical analysis, subjective experiences and sociocultural context are not recognised. Similarly, Schneider and Conrad (1980) argued that more research is needed into how illness is experienced within a social context.

Gerhardt (1989) highlighted that with the increasing prevalence of people suffering from a variety of chronic illnesses, it is important to understand the psychological and social aspects, and a qualitative method is necessary to explore personal meanings of living with a chronic illness, particularly because social adaptation and the quality of life of sufferers is vital to medical care. Radley (1999) asserted that psychology can make a valuable contribution to the redefinition of the patient as a person through the use of qualitative methods because of the emphasis it places on direct communication with individuals.

1.2.3 Responses to chronic illness

Although the experience of chronic illness is subject to sociocultural and historical influences, the sufferer is still required to live and function with his or her ailment amidst a generally healthy population (Radley, 1997). This requires a dynamic process of adjustment and adaptation to ongoing problems and disruptions in daily living.

It is essentially viewed as a problem to be solved through the adoption of adaptive strategies which enhance coping. The construction of meaning is identified by Fife (1994) as a central aspect in the adaption to illness. It refers to the individual's perception of their relationship to the world and is inextricably linked to identity. This is because meaning provides the sufferer with a sense of the coherence of life in the face of loss and change. The meaning a person gives to illness, in turn, influences the coping strategies adopted.

Success in coping can vary with the exacting nature of the illness, such as the type of onset; symptom intrusiveness, severity, and frequency; and changes in physical appearance. A positive response entails the maintenance of a valued premorbid lifestyle and a valued self-perception. However, the majority of studies suggest that some form of psychological distress can be a common experience for people who live with a chronic illness. In a review of recurrent themes in illness experience research, Conrad (1987) pinpointed a number of significant concepts and concerns which individuals described. These included feelings of uncertainty, stigma, identity negotiation, management of medical regimens, the need for information awareness and sharing, and finally family and social problems. It is generally agreed that the experience of any chronic illness has the potential to affect any aspect of everyday life. Research has helped in the understanding of typical problems encountered and shared by individuals living with enduring illness.

1.3 Social identity and self-concept in chronic illness

It is widely held that one of the consequences of chronic illness upon the individual is the impact and threat to self-concept and social identity (Conrad, 1987). The concepts have been discussed within a social context because chronic illness can result in a number of losses, for example, loss of a once healthy person, and restrictions related to status and employment (Charmaz, 1987).

INTRODUCTION

These restrictions and losses are closely linked to social identity, which represents the public and shared aspect of the individual. It is social identity that establishes the individual's position within the social structure.

Kelly and Field (1996) drew upon a symbolic interactionist perspective in their assertion that both social concept and self-concept are central 'to human social conduct', as well as being intrinsically related to the body. They describe the self-concept as a dynamic cognitive construct consisting of a set of perceptions and beliefs about oneself which is linked to the body and experienced as one entity. However, with chronic illness, a divergence occurs between the desired self-presentation and bodily demands. The body aspect of the person, which was once taken for granted, particularly within a social context, ceases to be taken for granted when it malfunctions.

Charmaz (1983) described the 'loss of self' in chronic illness as a fundamental form of suffering in the chronically ill. This is due to the erosion of the premorbid self by the progress of and conditions imposed by the debilitating illness. Charmaz noted that as a result of illness, individuals may be forced to lead restricted lives, which undermine a sense of personal freedom, choice, and control. These losses are made worse by values of independence and individual responsibility, which are held in high esteem by Western society. Socially the individual may become restricted and isolated as he or she may be faced with feeling discredited, ignored, and embarrassed and consequently withdraw. Finally, the individual may fear that he or she may come to be a burden to others, leading to the loss of independence and social isolation. However, one's entire self-concept and social identity are not necessarily lost in the face of chronic illness. Kelly and Field (1996) highlighted that whilst self-concept and social identity are dynamic processes, an enduring quality can be maintained as the person retains a sense of how he or she was before his or her body changed. Similarly, Bury (1982) describes chronic illness as a 'biographical disruption', where the challenge of the individual is to contextualise the illness experience, come to terms with the illness, and integrate it into a reconstituted self-concept.

1.3.1 Identity control in chronic illness

In a theoretical review, Gerhardt (1989) made a distinction between two ideas concerning self-concept and social identity, particularly in relation to the ability to manage social identity. One school of thought, the 'crisis model', refers to those illnesses for which identity change is unavoidable. Because the condition is not visible, this leads to societal reactions. The 'negotiation model', in contrast, provides an account of those illnesses which do not necessarily make a sufferer look ill. The physical symptoms do not necessarily impinge on interactions with others so are not taken into the social realm. However, the illness experience is still very real to the individual. This model characterizes chronic illness as imposing changes to the self-concept as the individual attempts to maintain and control a normal social identity.

1.4 The experience of stigma in chronic illness

Stigma is a socioculturally defined concept. In contemporary Western societies, it is used in a broad sense to refer to social disgrace associated with behaviours, attributes, and conditions. The morally loaded term *disgrace* implies that the individual is set aside as different, which holds the negative connotation of deviance (Scambler, 1984). Illness has consistently been regarded in early literature to be a state of deviance because of the threat it poses to social order. For example, it poses a threat to cultural norms which govern social interaction, that is, how much the illness interferes with the flow of interaction.

INTRODUCTION

The 'good' deviant is expected to contain 'bodily eruptions' in order to retain a credible status so as to save others from embarrassment (Goffman,1963) and maintain the flow of interaction. Hence, the main problem confronting the stigmatised individual who wants to be 'good' is the management of impressions that others may develop of him or her.

The extent of visibility of the bodily signs producing the stigma is a related factor (Goffman, 1986). If the source of stigma is overt, then the person is defined as 'discredited'. If it is concealable from others, then the stigma is experienced as 'discreditable'. In stigmatised disorders, regardless of whether they are visible or concealable, the stigma can begin with a societal reaction of disconfirmation and degradation of the individual. Eventually, the individual comes to expect these reactions, anticipating them before they may or may not occur. At this point, the stigma has been internalised by the individual in a sense of shame, self-discreditation, and spoiled identity. A vicious cycle ensues as the individual's behaviour becomes shaped by the negative perception of self (Kleinman, 1988).

A further distinction has been made between enacted and felt stigma. The former refers to discrimination based on the social unacceptability of the condition; the latter refers to feelings of shame and the fear that the stigma may be enacted. It was suggested by Scambler (1984) that with discreditable stigma, the preferred policy of nondisclosure tends to be adopted in order to prevent enacted stigma. Ironically it was found that this very fear of enactment, which is eliciting disgust and rejection from others, resulted in higher levels of emotional distress and of guarding against exposure risks that cause stigma. Various studies have found the extent of felt/perceived stigma is related to decreased psychological well-being (Raguram et al., 1996), poorer physical health, and increased use of medical services in chronic illness.

1.4.1 Information disclosure

Illness does not occur in isolation from the rest of life. Everyday activities provide an ongoing context in which the experience of unwanted symptoms need to be addressed. When the individual desires to be normal and lead an ordinary life, the potential of stigma can be experienced as isolating. The primary problem facing the discreditable person is one of information control —whether or how the condition should be disclosed to others (Goffman, 1986)—in order to avoid enacted stigma. He suggested the main goal of the stigmatised person is being accepted by 'normal' people. The more that individuals present themselves as normal, the less likely they are to be discredited. He conceptualised 'covering' as a strategy to hide and deflect attention from the stigma, causing the person to pass for normal.

The term *stigma potential* was used by Schneider and Conrad (1980) for those conditions where knowledge of the discreditable stigma is limited to a few others. Within the context of epilepsy, the authors highlighted that strategies of information management were selective. The individual may conceal and disclose the condition interchangeably according to the given social context. The decided action is not necessarily related to preserving the individual's identity. It is aimed at preventing others from restricting the individual from normal social roles. It is also based on the individual's perception of the condition and previous experiences with others after disclosure and the nature of the relationships involved.

Schneider and Conrad also described two forms of disclosure. The first form is 'telling as therapy', which involves the externalisation of negative feelings related to the self, such as guilt and self-derogation, to close, supportive, and nonjudgemental individuals. This facilitates feedback, renegotiation of stigma, and redefinition of the condition.

INTRODUCTION

The second form of disclosure, 'preventing telling', is used when there is a probability that others will observe the occurrence of stigma, for example, epileptic seizure or urgency in needing the toilet. Sometimes this involves the provision of medical explanation for the condition in an attempt to reduce the risk of stigmatisation. A motivating factor for this disclosure is to educate the members of society about the condition so as to remove the mystery and secrecy.

The authors demonstrated that disclosing can serve the same purpose as concealing in that both can consciously minimise the potentially negative impact on the individual's life.

Individuals diagnosed with the same condition and sharing similar experiences are isolated from one another. Schneider and Conrad (1980) noted that within the wilder culture, there tends to be a lack of illness subculture. This means the individuals remain separate from the other sufferers, and this is compounded by the desire to lead a normal, stigma-free life. Support groups can emerge as a means of support and provision of coping skills.

1.5 Coping with chronic illness

Coping behaviours refer to the cognitive, emotional, and behavioural actions employed by an individual in the face of an event. Chronic illness has been described in the literature as a stressful life event, as the impact on the individual's life can be tremendous. Living with chronic illness requires management and active adaption in many areas. In addition, a distinction is made between adaptive and maladaptive strategies, with the former having a positive effect and the latter serving to exacerbate the problems. However, it is recognised that coping is not a unidimensional concept and is difficult to define and cannot be measured simplistically. It functions at many levels and can be achieved through several different modes.

Five modes of coping were identified by Cohen and Lazarus (1983). These include the following:

a) Information seeking, i.e. learning about the problem in order to form a decision as to what can be done.
b) Direct actions, i.e. any action which aims to alter the person-environment favourably.
c) Inhibition of action, i.e. refraining from the temptation to exacerbate t situation by acting directly.
d) Intrapsychic processes, i.e. making a cognitive appraisal of the situation in an attempt to minimise distress.
e) Social support, i.e. turning to others to enhance individual efforts to de with the stressful event.

They suggested that the coping behaviours adopted by the chronically ill depend on the meanings assigned to the illness by the individual (which are in turn affected by social processes). This and the heterogeneous presentation of chronic illness accounts for the diversity of coping styles utilised by individuals. For example, a widely reported psychological coping strategy is one of denial, which can be constructed as a positive or negative form of coping. If the individual will not accept the condition, then he or she may try to continue with his or her life as if he or she did not have the illness. Other psychological strategies which are considered to be of little benefit to the individual include self-blame, shame, depression, and giving up.

Kleinman (1988) argued that seemingly maladaptive coping strategies may in fact help/aid cognitive appraisal of a stressor. In theorising on the effects of traumatic life events such as TIDM on personal beliefs, the author argued that successful coping involves making adjustments to schemas (which are internal cognitive structures) related to the self and the world.

INTRODUCTION

This involves the assimilation of the traumatic experiences into existing cognition and/or accommodating the experience by changing basic schemas. This integration of new information is made gradually so that a sense of stability is maintained through the process of adjustment. According to Kleinman, negative coping strategies such as self-blame and more positive strategies such as positive reinterpretations of the stressful event can facilitate this process of adaptation.

1.5.1 Coping through control

Kelly and Field (1996) proposed that a fundamental prerequisite for a social being is the physical body and its functions. Implicit in being in control is the sense of consistency it brings to the self-concept, as well as the ability to plan and predict. In order to perform competently within a social capacity, one must present control over the body. However, in chronic illness, the failure of the body means control cannot be taken for granted. Therefore, Kelly and Field suggest that the coping task which confronts the individual is dealing with the physical symptoms, thereby retaining a sense of control.

Research on locus of control has been largely influenced by Rotter's social learning theory (1966) and has been widely used in studies to predict the responses of those with chronic illness. A distinction is made between those who believe they can control outcomes via personal efforts (internal control) and those who believe in fate and luck and believe that external powers such as doctors control outcomes (external control). A belief that the illness and its symptoms are controllable is more likely to result in more effective management than beliefs of uncontrollability.

Findings as to whether the internal or external locus of control is more beneficial have been inconclusive, particularly within the context of chronic illness because adaptation is a complex, long-term process. It is mediated by many variables which have a direct impact on the individual who is learning to cope. Control cannot be viewed simply as an isolated personality characteristic (Cohen and Lazarus, 1989). As discussed earlier, coping through information—'passing for normal'—can help preserve the individual's social identity, which is facilitated by coping through symptom control.

1.6 TIDM as a chronic illness

TIDM is by identifying chronic hyperglycaemia, which is highly raised blood glucose accompanied by symptoms such as recent loss of weight, tiredness, excessive thirst, and increased urination (Williams and Pickup, 1999). The condition is caused by insulin deficiency, which results from progressive autoimmune destruction of insulin-producing beta cells in the pancreas. Diabetic ketoacidosis leading to may result if insulin is not replaced immediately.

There is no medical cure, but individuals are treated with injections of insulin, which is a hormone that lowers blood glucose, in order to survive. The condition is sometimes referred to as insulin-dependent diabetes mellitus (IDDM).

Behavioural modification is necessary, that is avoiding certain foods, engaging in regular exercise, doing capillary blood tests in order to monitor the condition, and submitting to regular medical check-ups to ensure good control. This shows that TIDM is both a physical and a psychosocial condition, and therefore it requires self-management and coping strategies by the individual. This may lead to an increased feeling of anxiety or depression, particularly if the difficulties of the individual experience with blood glucose control or develops complications (Lloyd, Dyer, and Barnett, 2000).

TIDM can be seen as a chronic endocrine disorder that can be controlled. The age of onset is similar for both girls and boys, but the pubertal peak occurs earlier in girls. TIDM is common during childhood to young adulthood, though it may occur at all ages.

1.6.1 TIDM as a chronic disorder

TIDM has been defined as a chronic disorder commonly caused by the autoimmune deconstruction of the beta cells of the pancreas. Severe insulin deficiency results in hyperglycaemia and ketoacidosis, which requires insulin replacement. Coma leading to death may result from potentially avoidable or treatable hyperglycaemia with insulin or hypoglycaemia if too much insulin was given, if no or little food was eaten, and if too much exercise was undertaken without an extra snack. The individual living with TIDM is expected to modify his or her lifestyle as pointed out by Williams and Pickup (1999), who argue that management encompasses a package of measures which include 'physiological' insulin injection regimes, assessment of control (usually home blood glucose monitoring and hospital tests of control), insulin adjustments, a healthy diet, adequate exercise, and diabetes education. The physiological symptoms cause emotional distress (Katon, 1984) arising from fear of the outcomes and response to chronic illness. This is different from hypochondria, which is based on beliefs related to fear of illness rather than actual symptoms.

Chronic disorders such as TIDM present a challenge to the contemporary medical model arising from the psychosocial results of living with the condition. According to the Cartesian model of mind-body dualism, there is an assumption that a problem resides either in the mind or in the body and that all hypotheses must be capable of being verified under objective empirical conditions. This model is appropriate when the symptoms presented can be objectively measured and are diagnosed as a disease.

It is well documented that the individual will seek an explanation for the cause of the illness as a coping strategy to gain some (Donoghue and Siegel, 2000). Beliefs about symptoms influence the illness experience, illness management, and interactions with health professionals and society. The individual is sometimes blamed for the illness and stigmatised by society.

1.6.2 The invisibility of TIDM

TIDM is one of the invisible chronic conditions (Donoghue and Siegel, 2000). The chronic illnesses in this subgroup are generally characterised by chronic symptoms which are not manifested externally. Therefore, the sufferer appears to be well despite living with a baseline of illness which is interrupted by periods of exacerbation and remission. This combined with a number of seemingly unconnected symptoms means the individual can be confronted by disbelief and suspicion from others. As a result, the sufferer not only has to cope with difficult and embarrassing symptoms but also is likely to endure negative societal reactions. In the face of these demands and tensions, living with an invisible chronic illness can have devastating consequences on the psychosocial well-being of many sufferers.

1.6.3 The causes and management of TIDM

The causes of TIDM remain unclear, particularly in the absence of any organic basis. Diet, lifestyle, remote childhood trauma (Williams and Pickup, 1999), and psychological factors have most commonly been suggested as the cause. The stress hypothesis implies some responsibility on the part of the individual. If the cause of TIDM is environmental factors, then the solution for preventing a recurrence and becoming healthy so as to prevent untoward effects such as diabetic ketoacidosis or severe hypoglycaemia may be seen to rest upon the sufferer.

INTRODUCTION

This means that the individual feels he or she should be able to control it but inevitably fails, leading to feelings of blame and guilt (Dancey and Backhouse, 1997). Charmaz (1983) stated that the individual experiences a feeling of loss of self, fear, and restriction when living with a chronic illness.

1.7 The experience of stigma in TIDM

First, the condition of TIDM raises discreditable stigma because it is invisible, as opposed to a public, visible discredited stigma. In Western society, illness of an organic origin is generally regarded as an accident, which leads to the sufferer being regarded as a victim. Moral connotations become attached to functional disorders as the individual is deemed responsible for the psychological distress which is not understood by the medical model, which places an emphasis on the cure for all illness. In such a case, the condition is likely to be defined as mysterious, and this brings with it moral judgements levelled against the sufferer. Second, the symptoms of hypoglycaemia are considered socially undesirable and consequently are the source of considerable embarrassment.

Kelly (1991), in the study of coping with an ileostomy (related to lack of control over bowels, which is invisible), described three means through which stigma is managed. Some patients may withdraw from social relationships because they are overwhelmed by the threat the consequences of stigma pose, and others may seek to conceal their condition in an effort to pass as normal. A final strategy is to 'come out' by announcing the condition and accepting it as a component of life, not the central focus. It is possible that these findings may be generalised to people with TIDM as noted in epilepsy by Schneider and Conrad (1980) in two forms of disclosure, that is, telling of therapy to receive support and choosing not to tell until people observe a seizure.

1.8 Methodological issues in TIDM research

Kelly and Field (1996) highlighted that the amount of research on common illnesses which have high prevalence rates and take up a large proportion of doctors' time was disproportionately less than the amount done on rarer illnesses such as HIV/AIDS. This observation is applicable to the limited research on TIDM. To date, the majority of research on TIDM has utilised quantitative measures to examine variables such as health-seeking behaviours, the role of stress, and personality characteristics. As noted previously, findings have been inconsistent and inconclusive, highlighting the stereotypical view that individuals with TIDM are a difficult patient group.

Another area on which research has focused is the relationship between TIDM and psychological distress. Again, inconclusive results have been obtained through the use of standardised measures, meaning it is difficult to form any firm conclusions. This is compounded by the distinction made between those who do and those who do not consult their health team regularly. Findings have suggested that psychological factors may be related to patient status rather than to the disorder per se. However, it is generally acknowledged that symptoms cannot be successfully managed at a purely physical level. The role of psychological therapies in effective treatment is increasingly being recognised (Raguram et al., 1996), given that there is no organic cause.

1.9 Focus of current research

Bury (1982) noted that individuals who have to manage illness that involves embarrassing changes in bodily function have particular difficulties in coping as chronic illness is a process of loss of normal as the individual struggles to be as normal as possible.

INTRODUCTION

This may lead to feelings of self-consciousness and stigmatisation (Scrambler, 1984), which can be compounded by the relative lack of recognition by medical professionals (Kleinman, 1988). The resulting trivialisation, as TIDM is not a life-threatening condition, means the quality of care provided to the sufferer is affected.

The person's ability to cope with the impact that the illness has on his or her life is vital for successful management. Conrad (1987) suggested there have been few studies on perception and strategies for managing conditions that are not overtly stigmatised. Research on chronic illness has acknowledged that common themes relating to living with the condition occur; there are also demands and experiences unique to each illness. An in-depth exploration of problems associated with TIDM is necessary, and it is important to understand how sufferers make sense of their condition, the label that it is chronic, and the explanation given by health professionals.

1.9.1 Research aims

The following research questions were in mind in order to understand how adolescents diagnosed with TIDM make sense of and experience living with the condition:

1) How do adolescents describe their experiences of living with TIDM a cope with it?
2) How do adolescents experience and perceive the stigma of living with TIDM?
3) How do adolescents manage the experiences and stigma while interacting/negotiating with the society of which they are a part?

Qualitative research was used to obtain the perspective of a small sample of adolescents living with T1DM. The study aimed to contribute to psychosocial aspects and to broaden the professionals' understanding of some of the demands of living with T1DM. This research may also help adolescents to provide further information about the meaning and outcomes of living with T1DM, a sense of empowerment, and increased coping skills.

1.9.2 Rationale

During adolescence, there is a need to define self whilst attempting to conform to peer group activities such as going to late-night parties or clubs, engaging in vigorous sports, and experimenting with recreational drugs and alcohol. During this period, adolescents are expected to internalise societal norms of adulthood, cope with demands of health/illness, and still appear 'normal' to the public. It is a unique physical, psychosocial, and transitional period from childhood to adulthood. Any chronic condition like type 1 diabetes mellitus adds another burden and more pressure as some adolescents are starting to be more independent of parental care, or have left their homes to study at colleges/universities or travel abroad or have started to work. Others are dating with the hope of forming a permanent relationship, planning a family, and having their own home.

2

Method

This section presents a description and justification for the research methodology adopted. An overview and the rationale for using the qualitative approach and a description of grounded theory will be discussed. Details of procedures involved in data collection, participants, and the interview guide will be included. Finally, a framework for data analysis will be described, and reliability and validity will be discussed.

2.1 The qualitative approach

One of the primary aims of this qualitative research is to understand the experiences of adolescents living with type 1 diabetes mellitus (TIDM) and what they encounter during their interactions with society. Strauss and Corbin (1990) defined the methodology of the qualitative strategy as any research that does not involve the use of procedures that are quantifiable or statistical analysis. There is a contrast between qualitative and quantitative analyses. The latter is an experimental, positivist approach based on the concept that reality is presented as objective facts. The aim is to explain the causal relationship via the control of variables in relation to a predetermined theory.

Numerous subjects are involved, and the responses are allocated into predetermined categories to obtain broad and generalised results.

In qualitative research, the approach is interpretative and descriptive. The qualitative method is based on the phenomenological description. This is the idea that another's beliefs, intentions, perspectives, feelings, and so forth can be revealed to the interviewer, who acts in a neutral way and presupposes nothing (Patton, 1980). There is a search for meaning and description within the context of the identified phenomenon. Reality is represented through the perception of the participants in their subjective responses. The researcher aims to define themes, find out emerging concepts, and categorise data of their experiences. This approach engages a smaller number of participants to provide an in-depth and detailed account of their experiences.

2.1.1 Rationale for using qualitative method

Recognition of the value of qualitative research in the field of chronic illness and health psychology has increased dramatically over the past few years. The shift has been influenced by evidence that the medical model (based on mind-body dualism and positivism) has not provided in-depth explanations as to how illness is experienced and managed by those who live with it. A combination of biological, psychological, and social factors, and what individuals experience, needs to be considered to fully understand a chronic condition. Yardley (1997) and Radley (1999) stated that quantitative research in illness could not be used to explore individual feelings and experiences effectively.

There is not enough research on living and coping with TIDM, particularly in relation to perceived stigma. Strauss and Corbin (1990) propose that qualitative methods can be used to explore, generate hypotheses, and gain new insights into phenomena of which little is known.

This method can provide a means by which an understanding of the individual's experience of living and coping with chronic illness can be attempted. In contrast, Radley (1999) noted that quantitative methods focus on objectifying illness using predetermined scales and questionnaires. Here the emphasis is on an attempt to verify predetermined hypotheses relating to the illness phenomena rather than exploration and generation of insights.

In this study, the exploratory aim is to obtain subjective accounts from the adolescents' perspective of living with TIDM. It was noted in the introduction that research on the chronic illness of a quantitative nature is expanding, and these studies measure variables such as emotional distress and satisfaction. This study aimed to explore the TIDM experience, which would be difficult to carry out with objective measures. Qualitative methods are suitable to study the experiences of coping with this condition and possible perceived stigma. It is hoped that the qualitative nature of this study will help to bring new insights to professionals' understanding of issues related to living with TIDM.

2.2 Grounded theory

The grounded theory approach was developed by Glaser and Strauss in the 1960s partly to present a view of the chronic illness experience of people dying in hospitals. It has been adopted within the psychological health field as a methodological tool particularly suited to the study of chronic illness (Charmaz, 1990). Of the many qualitative methods, the grounded theory involves a systemic set of data collection analytic procedures aimed at the generation of a theory. The theory is described as grounded in the data (i.e. the participant's own accounts of his or her experience and socio-psychological processes). This is because the researcher analyses what he or she obtains in data rather than being bounded by preconceived hypotheses.

Grounded theory is influenced theoretically by symbolic interactionism, a framework that is based on the assumption that individuals ascribe meanings to their worlds that evolve from shared social interactions (Charmaz, 1990). The dynamic process is achieved by negotiation, reflexivity, and interpretation. Hence, the emphasis is that people are not passive reactors to incoming information but respond actively and creatively to perceptions of reality. These perceptions are constantly being created and recreated according to the meaning given to the situation as well as to the response negotiated from the interaction.

With the flexibility offered by the method of grounded theory, personal meanings can be explored and contextual psychology and social process, which are developed to facilitate sense-making, can be elicited. It is described as an inductive strategy for obtaining a theory that emerges from the examined phenomenon. This implies a simultaneous involvement in data collection and analysis, as initial hypotheses that emerge during the early stages of data collection can be incorporated into the design of further interviews. The position of the researcher in relation to the emerging data is that of an observer, whereby concepts will 'come out' as the reciprocal data collection and analysis proceed to the 'finding' of a theory.

2.2.1 Grounded theory revised

As grounded theory has evolved, numerous issues have led to a revision of the original approach. Charmaz (1990) claimed that the traditional methodology attempts to marry phenomenological and positivistic epistemologies. This has been described as confusing and inconsistent as the incorporation of the latter brings assumptions of the passivity of the research role. The concepts, categories, and theory reveal themselves from the data without the influence of the researcher.

This, suggests Charmaz, comes close to inferring an external reality 'from the outside in', which is contrary to the 'from the inside out' perspective upon which qualitative approaches are based.

Charmaz (1990) proposes that the process of research involves an active position of the researcher, who plays a part in coconstructing the participant's experiences. There is an interplay between the background of the researcher (i.e. values and perspective and the relationship with the participant). This serves to influence the reciprocal processes of data collection and analysis. For example, it is the researcher's theoretical stance that will affect the types of questions asked as well as provide a base from which the questions are framed to provide a great depth of data.

2.3 Ethical issues

In accordance with the professional guidelines, ethical approval was sought from the Local Ethics Research Committee of the health authority where the researcher worked when undertaking the study. It was anticipated that the study would not propose any ethical concerns for the participants. However, it was considered that the interviews might prompt discussion of topics that could be upsetting to participants. It was proposed that in such an event, the participant would be given the opportunity to discuss this, and information would be provided by the researcher regarding sources of support. There were no potential risks and hazards associated with the study, but in anticipation of short-term emotional distress, the psychologist was aware and supportive of the study being undertaken. He agreed to offer intervention as needed.

2.3.1 Ethical approval

Permission from the consultant physician for adolescents with TIDM was sought and obtained. Informed consent was provided for each participant. It was explained that participation was voluntary and that nonparticipation and withdrawal from the study would not affect individuals at the diabetic clinic. An information sheet explaining the aim of the study, a consent form, and a cover letter were sent to each invited participant.

2.3.2 Anonymity and confidentiality

Anonymity and confidentiality were maintained by conducting individual interviews, and participants' names and addresses were not used. Personal data were not stored in the computer to prevent the identification of participants, and electronic interviews were avoided for the same reason. Information was not disclosed to anyone, and collected data were kept in a locked cupboard at the researcher's home. Privacy and confidentiality were ensured by not checking participants' medical records, their diabetes control, and their attendance at the clinic against their responses. The data would be destroyed after analysis (Data Protection Acts of 1994 and 1998). Each participant was interviewed on a different day to avoid any meeting or recognition by another participant. The name of the hospital or the diabetic clinic was not mentioned. Deception would be avoided by communicating true results and by not giving misleading information about the study to the participants. The published results of the study in a local hospital magazine or an appropriate professional journal will be available to participants on request.

2.4 Design

Individual interviews face-to-face were suitable because the researcher needed to collect subjective information from verbal interchange from a small sample because of the time factor and economic reasons. Adolescents appreciated more privacy and did not wish to talk in piloting focus groups, except for two who tended to be outspoken and dominating. In epilepsy, Schneider and Conrad (1980) highlighted that strategies of information were selective and that the individual may conceal his or her condition interchangeably, according to the given social context, not preserving the individual's identity. The biomedical care of people living with a chronic condition has not explained fully how illness is experienced and managed daily psychosocially (e.g. in self-identity and with regard to the concept of stigma). The interviews were face-to-face with verbal interchanges and electronic recordings simultaneously. Mental notes were taken, written notes were made promptly after each interview, and feedback was requested from each respondent to ensure accuracy. Interviews were conducted at the place of the respondent's choice. Costs of travel to and from the location were reimbursed.

2.4.1 Sampling

The sample was convenient because it included adolescents who were already attending the district diabetic clinic where the researcher was employed. This proved economical as the travelling distance was short. With the help of the Diabetes Register, it was easy to get the names of the intended participants from a database who had a similar social background. Invitation letters were sent to sixty-nine adolescents between the ages of sixteen and nineteen years of age. It was a normal distribution sample representing both males and females living with TIDM for two to fifteen years.

This yielded thirteen volunteers, which resulted in a nonrepresentative population for the study.

The invitation letter which motivated each participant to take part and to state how he or she felt about the study was sent to the adolescents with TIDM attending the clinic (Gillham, 2000, in Denzin and Lincoln, 2000). An interview schedule, an information sheet, a consent form, and self-addressed prepaid stamped envelopes were sent to willing respondents. They were requested to respond in two weeks' time, but very few met the deadline. Therefore, a second mailshot was sent one week after the closing date to all intended participants as a reminder. Twenty-one adolescents responded, and a total of thirty-four volunteers returned the consent forms.

2.4.2 Criteria for participation

Participants had a formal diagnosis of TIDM by a qualified medical practitioner, and they were to be on insulin injection prescribed by the medical doctor for the treatment of their condition. As all participants had lived with their condition for more than a year, this ensured that they would be able to provide adequate experiences and full perception of living with TIDM. Outpatients were recruited in order to exclude extreme experiences of TIDM and to provide a natural setting for participants as recommended by Conrad (1990). The age range was sixteen to nineteen years as literature has shown that it is within this age group when adolescents experience the transitional period from childhood to adulthood and are going through significant changes both physically and psychosocially (Williams and Pickup, 1999). It is the stage of significant changes such as finishing high school education, starting at college/university, dating, forming new relationships, perhaps starting a family and a job, and possibly engaging in risk-taking behaviour.

Still, they are expected to cope with the daily management of TIDM (Carson, 2001; Ng, Darko, and Hillson, 2002).

2.4.3 Adolescents excluded from the study

The researcher aimed at understanding the language and culture during interviews so as to interpret subjective data. Adolescents who did not understand English, those who used sign language and those with learning disabilities were excluded because there were no resources to deal with them, for example, interpreters or caregivers, and they could not give a full account of their experiences of living with TIDM.

2.4.4 Participants

All participants had a diagnosis of TIDM and were from all social classes and ethnic groups living in the district or the surrounding areas. They were males and females aged between sixteen and nineteen years. They were either completing high school education, at college/university or working full-time. There were nine participants, of which four were males and five were females. On receipt of all the completed consent forms, eleven respondents were randomly selected (names were drawn from a hat). Two volunteers withdrew from the study and did not turn up for the interview on the agreed day and time. The numbers were anticipated to be equal to represent the gender ratio of adolescents living with TIDM (Williams and Pickup, 1999). Participants were asked to sign consent forms in order to be included in the study. Nine volunteers were interviewed at a place and during the time of their choice. Their travelling expenses were reimbursed if necessary. Some participants have interviewed in their own homes, and most adolescents did not like to be interviewed at or near the hospital; therefore, a neutral venue had to be sought, e.g. a church hall.

After establishing rapport, a debriefing was done to ensure that each participant felt the same about himself or herself on arrival. The procedure to be followed was explained, demographics were taken, and then each participant was interviewed for one hour using the interview schedule in appendix 6. The participants were six Caucasians, two blacks, and one Asian, though ethnicity was not an issue in this study. The length of time since diagnosis of TIDM was from one year to fifteen years, and each participant suffered similar symptoms, namely excessive thirst, increased urination, tiredness, and loss of weight, except one who did not recognise the symptoms until she was in a coma and was treated at an intensive care unit of a hospital. Further probing was used when necessary, and participants were given the opportunity to offer additional information as required. The interview was recorded. The researcher made memory-jogging notes during the interview, and the tape was played to each interviewee to ensure accuracy, to add more information, and to avoid distortion of data (Kirk and Miller, 1986). The tape recordings were transcribed into a word processing package verbatim to enable the identification of themes.

2.4.5 Instruments

Standardised, semistructured open-ended questions were formulated for the interview schedule according to the topic of the study in order to answer research questions. Easy questions were asked first about self, the attitude of the health professionals, and perceived stigma by society. The questions allowed probing on required information (Patton, 1980) as some participants did not say much, simply responding with a yes or no to a question. Pilot testing of the instrument had been done to address issues such as the validity of each question, clarification of word meaning and instructions, systematic questioning, and relevant issues (Gillham, 2000).

The participants were given an opportunity to ask questions or add any relevant information at the end of the interview. Contact telephone numbers and names of health personnel who could offer help in case of need, for example, the consultant physician, the psychologist, and the diabetes specialist nurse, were provided for each participant.

2.5 Qualitative data collection and analysis

Data collection and analysis in this study was conducted within the constructionist framework proposed by Charmaz (1996). Therefore, the categories developed from an analysis of the data will be informed by an interaction between the theoretical background of the researcher and the participants' accounts of their experience of living with TIDM. This constructionist approach will be used in conjunction with the general guidelines of the qualitative method, and a wide range of different conflicting statements that were noted. Silverman (1999) suggested that a face-to-face individual interview was preferred to telephone or electronic interviews to ensure anonymity and privacy of the participants. He also mentioned the issue of disclosure where some participants may be dominating and others keeping quiet or saying very little during the whole interview. Qualitative research is a chosen method to collect and analyse subjective data, which in this case are experiences of living with TIDM and the perception of stigma by the adolescents.

2.5.1 Data collection

On receipt of all the completed consent forms, respondents were randomly selected (their names were drawn from a hat). All randomly selected volunteers who had consent forms were included in the study. Two volunteers withdrew from the study before interviews, and nine volunteers were interviewed at a place and during a time of their choice.

Each participant was interviewed for one hour using the interview schedule in appendix 6 and including demographics. Further probing was used when necessary, and participants were given the opportunity to offer additional information as required. The interview was recorded, and the researcher made memory-jogging notes to prevent distraction during the interview. The notes were written down while the memory was still fresh to avoid distortion of data. The recording was checked back with each respondent to clarify ambiguity. The tape recordings were transcribed into a word processing package to enable the identification and emerging themes.

2.5.2 Data analysis

In order to turn the recorded interviews into a permanent record from which analysis could proceed, a transcript of the oral information into written form was necessary. Following transcription, coding was conducted in order to define the data. It has been described by Strauss and Corbin (1990) as the process by which data is broken down, examined, and reassembled to give a new meaning for analysis of qualitative data vis-à-vis grounded theory methodology. The researcher used Patton's (1980) approach to qualitative analysis. Using grounded theory is generated by induction of data that is first categorised on the basis of content, avoiding any theoretical presuppositions, and then by developing links between categories. Data were coded according to positive and negative themes, and vague and meaningless data were not coded.

2.5.2.1 Line-by-line coding

Also known as open coding (Strauss and Corbin, 1990), line-by-line coding represents the first step in data analysis as proposed by Charmaz (1990), and it facilitates making comparisons of responses.

It involves the examination of each line of data and descriptive labelling (preferably in the participants' terms) of each event being talked about by the participant. Here an interaction between the data and researcher occurs, as questions are asked of the phenomenon being verbalised by the participant. Answers to questions such as 'What is happening?' and 'What is the participant doing or saying?' help break the data into categories and facilitate the recognition of processes, actions, and beliefs that occur in the data. This provided a deeper understanding of the experiences and perceived stigma by adolescents living with TIDM.

This process was conducted with an awareness of how the researcher's view would influence the definitions in the data. It is acknowledged that whilst the label given to a concept should provide a recognisable description of the phenomena, the researcher's discipline will have an impact on the codes that are created.

2.5.2.2 Focused coding

This next stage takes the concepts derived from line-by-line coding and refines them into increasingly abstract higher-level categories. Strauss and Corbin (1990) labelled this phase of analysis as *axial coding* whereby the data is reassembled. It is a process that is less open-ended and more directed, as analysis is more selective and conceptual. Those codes which continually appeared in the line-by-line coding are used to 'sift' through the remainder of the text. As the volume of the data increases, analytic categories are developed to cover common themes derived from several codes. Charmaz (1995) suggested that the categories may be 'in vivo codes' taken directly from the discourse of the interviewee, or they may represent the researcher's substantive definition of what is happening.

Charmaz (1995) suggested that a number of comparisons of similarities and differences should be made in the data as a part of the process of focused coding. These include comparing different people, comparing categories, and comparing the same participant's account at different points in time. This process is known as constant comparison and aims to seek similarities, differences, and relationships between categories in order to build and clarify the category. The aim of this process is to link and integrate categories in order to account for variations and establish a pattern of the data.

2.5.2.3 Selective coding

Strauss and Corbin recommended a final stage of analysis, selective coding. This refers to the process of integrating and bridging the theory. The researcher aims to identify one or more core categories that tie together the other categories in the theory.

2.5.2.4 Memo writing

In parallel to the coding process, Charmaz (1990) advised the use of theoretical memos to facilitate the elaboration of processes and definitions within the data. The process continues to make use of constant comparison between and within participants as the analysis becomes more abstract as it progresses. Memo writing involves taking the categories apart in order to trace the process of category formation. Category definition occurs through the identification of its properties (i.e. category characteristics), examining underlying assumptions and showing how it changes and evolves. Through this process, Charmaz (1990) stated that the researcher can look for implicit meanings in the data. Theoretical sampling should lead on from memo writing. This is where the researcher might revisit the interviewees in order to collect more data with a view to clarifying the emerging theory. The process again utilised constant comparisons as concepts were refined. Ideally, the process of data collection and analysis continues until no new categories can be identified and the goal of theoretical is achieved.

3

Results

3.1 Demography of participants

The mean age of adolescents who took part in the study was eighteen years. Duration of TIDM was mostly between six and ten years. Two participants were diagnosed with TIDM at the age of two years, and only one had had TIDM for nearly two and a half years. It was noted that there were more adolescents of Caucasian origin as compared to Asians and blacks, though the study was not looking at ethnic issues. The gender ratio was acceptable. Out of nine participants, four were in high school, two at college, only one at university, one working, and one not yet employed. They were all living with their parents, except one who lived with a friend. One participant was pregnant. All participants had experienced the symptoms of the condition, and those who were diagnosed at a very young age were told about similar symptoms by their parents. One participant did not recognise the symptoms until she was in a coma and taken to hospital at the age of twelve years.

They were all on insulin injection two to four times a day and were doing a series of blood glucose tests in order to maintain diabetes control.

Regular medical check-ups and clinic visits were scheduled, and these were more frequent in pregnancy and uncontrolled TIDM.

3.2 Interview extracts

In the extracts, it is shown that living with TIDM did not bother some of the participants, whereas others expressed worry and concern most of the time. In common with other chronic illnesses and traumatic life events, TIDM and its management impose a considerable burden of psychological stress which needs to be coped with through adaptation until satisfactory solutions are found (Williams and Pickup, 1999). A study done to evaluate the factors that influence the quality of life in adolescents with TIDM concluded that the diabetes treatment team needed to pay equal attention to psychosocial aspects (Grey et al., 1998). This was confirmed by Faro (1999), who reported that the theme of adaptation was expressed most often by participants who had had diabetes for a long period of time. Another study on the prevalence of psychological symptoms in adults older than eighteen years showed that 28 per cent of participants reported moderate to severe levels of depression or anxiety or both (Lloyd, Dryer, and Barnett, 2000). The following extracts also confirmed the previous findings.

- Participants' statements about self-identity:
- 'Living with diabetes is like a nightmare. It really makes me worry every day.'
- 'Diabetes is a horror, and I'm very angry that I have it because I have schoolwork as well.'
- 'Why and how did I get it after all? My brother and sister complain about the more attention I get from Mom and Dad.'

RESULTS

- 'I'm really upset and fed up about this. I think of injections and nice food can't go clubbing and skiing freely without my poor dad fussing.'
- 'Injections and pricking my finger for the blood sugar test bother me a lot.'
- 'Why not use less painful gargets like insulin pumps or let me pancreas transplant?'
- 'I worry and I am afraid that I shall get hypoglycaemia and start to be like a nut.'
- 'It is embarrassing to have a low [hypoglycaemia].'
- 'It's a shame I am a boy with diabetes. My PE teacher always reminds me to take it easy in sport.'
- 'I am angry because diabetes has restricted me in sport and dating girls.'
- 'I am now temperamental and moody on most days. I think it is my diabetes which causes this.'
- 'Living with TIDM does not bother me; I know no other lifestyle, a diagnosed at two years of age.'
- 'Diabetes is my way of life, and it has taught me time management and more disciplined.'
- 'I now enjoy a healthy diet and regular exercise while controlling my sugar. Diabetes has no impact on my life. I'm just like any other teenager who goes to parties, and I'm involved in sport.'
- 'My life is more structured since I got diabetes, and I think I live happily.'
- 'I don't remember living without TIDM; therefore, it is like second nature.'
- 'There is no problem because I can eat sweet things sensibly and w blood sugar levels are low.'
- 'I know a girl who uses an insulin pump, but I'm still contented with injections.'

Patients' perceptions of health professionals' attitudes:

- 'Doctors and nurses are supportive, friendly, and caring.'
- 'Some doctors and nurses explain TIDM well, and others think you understand; therefore they leave you to search for more information on the condition.'
- 'They treat you as if you are "thick" at times. It happens when you come to hospital as a result of uncontrolled diabetes or hypoglycaemia.'
- 'My doctor always focuses on my diabetes even if I have to see him about other complaints. I don't want to be reminded that I have diabetes time.'
- 'Some show more sympathy to younger or pregnant people with diabetes 'I do not want to know what caused my diabetes, because it will not go away.'
- 'My doctor told me that maybe it was some viral infection I got or some genes.'

Participants' statements about the social stigma:

- 'It is embarrassing to inject at a restaurant or in front of your schoolmates every day. They become curious and ask you what [they can] do in help.'
- 'I keep my diabetes private because some people think you get it as so of punishment.'
- 'Members of society mistake you for a drunk when you suffer from blood sugar.'
- 'It is better that people cannot see that I have diabetes unless hypoglycaemia.'

- 'Some employers do not accept people living with TIDM. They think cause problems at work and that the individual will not give performance due to being unwell or absent.'
- 'Vigorous sports such as rugby and skydiving can be a problem.'
- 'Pretending to be "normal" can lead to little or no help if an emergency arises.'
- 'The society does not believe that one lives with TIDM, because there visible physical abnormalities. My classmates thought I liked to myself from school a lot.'
- 'My parents and teachers are protective and more vigilant as far as diabetes is concerned.'
- 'People need to know what to do so as to help a person with hypogly instead of panicking.'
- 'The public needs education on diabetes and about the different types rectify some beliefs and myths.'

In chronic illnesses such as ulcerative colitis which can be treated by radical surgery, the tension between self-presentation and socially constructed public identity may result (Kelly, 1992). The control of one's body's most basic function is transformed by surgery, and this condition is common in early adulthood when individuals have started courting or are already married and working. The same is for TIDM, where an individual controls blood glucose by a series of tests and insulin injections from an early age or during the transitional period from childhood to adulthood. The individual worries about the illness itself, any emergencies in case the regimen of treatment was omitted or delayed, type of food and activities in public, as well as outcomes of the condition. Private life becomes public when, during an interaction, people notice something is different from the individual and stigma is constructed (Goffman, 1989). The public may react positively or negatively (Kelly, 1992), and this becomes worse when people lack knowledge or have little knowledge about the condition. Identity is concerned with potential labelling, perceived assigning of stigma, and experience of power relation in social institutions. Counselling and providing information help individuals to cope with daily living with the illness.

4

Discussion

The aim of the study was to explore the experiences of adolescents living with TIDM and how they interact/negotiate with society. This study looked at their self-identity, the reaction of the public to the invisible chronic condition, and the perceived stigma. Experiences and coping skills during self-management of TIDM were also noted, as was the need for psychosocial support and counselling, as noted by Lloyd, Dyer, and Barnett (2000). The findings were similar to other studies which explored experiences and stigma perceived by the individuals living with chronic illnesses. Selective coding was done, and themes leading to the categories, namely assimilation and stigmatisation, were identified as experienced by most interviewees. The response is coping and adapting to illness as the condition affects the body and mind (Kleinman, 1988); therefore, psychosocial counselling needed to be borne in mind when managing TIDM.

There were some differences and similarities in experiences and stigma perception by the individuals living with TIDM among both male and female participants of all included ages.

There was no variation even among those who were still in full-time education or employment. The five modes of coping with chronic illness identified by Cohen and Lazarus (1983) were noted as some participants were keen to learn more about TIDM tried hard to keep the condition under control, concealed it by preventing the occurrence of either diabetic ketoacidosis or hypoglycaemia, or pretended there was nothing wrong in order to pass for normal. The same was noted by Dancey and Backhouse (1997) for people living with irritable bowel syndrome. Those who concealed TIDM were trying to deal with perceived stigma and to cope with the condition in their own way. Others disclosed TIDM and its related emergencies so that they could get support, sympathy, and acceptance by society, not just perceived stigma (Goffman, 1986).

The youngest participant seemed to be struggling with coping skills. He said: 'I can't freely enjoy sweets and chocolates anymore. Injections are painful. I am angry because diabetes has restricted me in sport and dating some girls, and my PE teacher always reminds me to take it easy. I have not told anyone that I have diabetes, and I know nobody who has diabetes.' These responses confirmed fear, a feeling of shame, and restriction cited by Charmaz (1983). Participants who were diagnosed at a very young age seemed to be coping well with the perceived stigma of living with TIDM. One participant responded: 'I don't remember my life without diabetes.' Another said: 'Diabetes is my second life.' These participants were coming to terms with the stigma of living with chronic illness as cited by Scambler and Hopkins (1986) in being epileptic, and they had accommodated TIDM in their daily lives. This helped to improve their coping skills, and they had conceptualised and adapted to chronic illness (Fife, 1994).

4.1 Self-identity

Most participants agreed that the symptoms of TIDM bothered them. One was ashamed of frequent visits to the toilet, which this individual still experienced when diabetes was out of control, though there was no body change (Bury, 1982). This condition made the participant feel different and not 'normal'. Inhibition of action was adopted as a mode of action cited by Cohen and Lazarus (1983). Some participants experienced embarrassment, which resulted in nondisclosure felt due to stigma described as deviance in Parson's sick role (Goffman, 1963; Scambler, 1984). Some expressed fear of diabetic or hypoglycaemic coma. The adolescent who had been in a coma felt very strong about being unconscious because of diabetes. They all felt that living with T1DM affected their lifestyles because they always needed to think before engaging in any activities, although two participants who were diagnosed as toddlers stated that diabetes did not bother them as they knew no other lifestyle. Living with T1DM made most of them unlike other teenagers, who only have to cope with physical and psychosocial development. As stated by Ingersoll (1989), during this period adolescents start to develop a sense of individual identity and self-worth whilst there is an alteration of body image. Adolescents start to adapt to more matured intellectual abilities, adjust to society's demands, internalise personal values, and prepare for adult roles.

4.2 Experiences of living with T1DM

Some participants were really bothered by living with T1DM, its daily management, and the possible untoward outcomes such as coma. This led to a feeling of fear, shame, and despondence as they perceived themselves as not the same as their peers, which made them feel like giving up as stated in Charmaz (1987).

Living with T1DM was seen as an extra burden that should not occur in their busy lifestyle. Restrictions in diet and times to follow the treatment regimen were also perceived as tiresome and demanding. T1DM had taken their freedom to eat anything they like and also prevented some male participants from partaking in a dangerous sport without taking precautions to prevent hypoglycaemia. Restriction by refraining from some foods and activities was another mode of coping with and accommodating chronic illness (Cohen and Lazarus, 1983). One participant demonstrated fear and horror by wishing for an injection-free period at least a continuous insulin infusion via a pump to make life easier for him. As has been expressed by Kleinman (1988), those suffering from serious and especially disabling chronic disorders desire to limit the sometimes dehumanising effects of a medicalised society and the effects of forms of medical treatment that deliver increasing technical sophistication but fail to offer 'comfort and care' for patients as whole human beings.

Female participants who were diagnosed with TIDM at a very young age and four of those who had it as teenagers stated that living with the condition did not bother them because they did not have to adapt in order to cope with the condition. All male participants except one were bothered by living with diabetes. Some participants perceived living with diabetes as a way of life that helped with discipline and organisation of structured everyday activities. Living with the condition was seen as a motivational and educational tool, and these participants viewed themselves as more mature, independent, knowledgeable, and self-reliant as compared to their peers.

Internal locus of condition (Rotter, 1966) was demonstrated by personal effort, and external locus control entailed the assistance of health professionals and support by family/friends to control TIDM. This demonstrated a positive way of adjusting to and coping with diabetes. There was negative feedback, such as TIDM restricted one in life as cited by Charmaz (1983 and 1987) in dating, in particular sports, and with regard to some jobs.

This was confirmed by one adolescent who mentioned that the public needed to be aware of the difference between TIDM and T2DM (type 2 diabetes mellitus) because they are different conditions and therefore the approach to management is not the same.

DISCUSSION

4.3 Stigma from health professionals

Most participants perceived stigma from health professionals whenever they consulted their doctors for something else, for example, pregnancy or a sore throat. The doctors or nurses started to discuss diabetes even if it was well controlled and seemed not to concentrate on the main complaint. The participants preferred to be accepted and treated as normal by medical professionals because they felt embarrassed by the perceived stigma of living with TIDM.

Viewing them as normal individuals as cited by Goffman (1986) helps them to adapt and cope with chronic illness. The stigma became worse if the blood glucose was high or extremely high or if there was an episode of severe hypoglycaemia. One participant stated that he dreaded Christmas parties for children with diabetes, saying that they were like nightmares to him because it seemed as parents, doctors, and nurses were observing who was eating a lot of 'forbidden' foods. Embarrassment and guilt, followed by an overreaction by members of society who do not understand psychological behaviour (Gerhardt, 1989), was noted in this study.

Restriction in life was accompanied by fear of condition outcomes, and loss of self-identity was noted as cited by Charmaz (1987). These two things were reported by most participants. Another participant had perceived no stigma and thought the health professionals were kind, supportive, and very caring towards children with diabetes, whether they were male or female. Older people were seen to be treated differently by some participants, especially those with T2DM because they were blamed for their not so good lifestyle at times.

The youngest male participant said: 'Doctors treat you as if you are "thick"', which indicated he did not bother with a cognitive appraisal related to distress while trying to cope as identified by Cohen and Lazarus (1983). The oldest female participant said: 'Some doctors explain so well that you are tempted to sit and listen even if you are in a hurry, but others seem to think you will not understand the difficult stuff.' This showed that the individual sometimes tried to cope and adjust by obtaining adequate information elsewhere about the condition (Dancey and Backhouse, 1997). The participant who expressed anger as far as TIDM was concerned stated that he did not want to listen to all of the information about the condition; he only wanted to know what to do in order to control diabetes and continue living. As reported by Donoghue and Siegel (2000), individuals living with invisible chronic illness are sick and tired of the symptoms; therefore, they seek explanations for how to cope with illness whilst interacting with society.

4.4 Social stigma

Some participants felt better that TIDM was invisible, but others wished it was obvious to the public that one was living with TIDM in case of an emergency such as hypoglycaemia. One participant had a nasty experience when members of the public thought he was under the influence of alcohol or some other drug during a severe hypoglycaemic attack that landed him in hospital. There was a perceived social stigma, especially when people did not understand TIDM, and they did not give the support and sympathy deserved. Two participants had lost friendships because of the condition, and one suspected that he was not offered a job when the prospective employer learnt that he had TIDM. About half the participants were of the opinion that society does not understand diabetes as a whole and education are necessary in order to explain the difference between the types of diabetes.

This showed the participants had adapted to living with the condition and how they coped whilst negotiating with the society, which still needed to be identified in other studies.

DISCUSSION

Females and younger people with TIDM were thought to be treated better by the majority, and especially the pregnant ones seemed to be more cared for by both health professionals and the public. Those who concealed their diabetic condition had a fear of being stigmatised and being treated as invalid because they were not particularly sick as in having an acute illness. As one participant stated: 'My brother and sister complain that I get more attention.' Another said: 'I can't go clubbing and skiing freely without my poor dad fussing.' Acceptance and denial of condition played major roles in the disclosure of the condition. Some adolescents stated that they were not keen to tell anyone about their invisible condition until it made sense to them and after they had adapted and learnt how to cope and how to live with diabetes. The assimilation process helped in telling friends and schoolmates about TIDM, and social unacceptability made others conceal the condition with the hope that there would be no diabetic emergencies.

4.5 Validity of the study

There are no standard means of assuring validity in qualitative research such as in quantitative measurements (Norman, Denzin, and Lincoln, 2000). The interview tape was played for each participant to ensure accuracy and comprehension and to prevent distortion during the interpretation of data. Verbatim quotes were used. These were transcribed to a word processor and proofread before coding. During the analysis of data, many themes were identified and concepts emerged. These were grouped into categories that demonstrated accuracy and consistency as shown in previous studies that explored experiences of living with chronic illnesses.

The categories identified were (*a*) sense-making/understanding of TIDM; (*b*) controlling the condition; (*c*) self-identity change; (*d*) invalidation/ lack of belief; (*e*) social unacceptability of TIDM; and (*f*) strategies for being normal. All these categories led to assimilation or accommodation of the condition and stigmatisation by society. Modes of coping with chronic illness as stated by Cohen and Lazarus (1983) were used during adaptation in TIDM.

4.5.1 Sensemaking/understanding

Most participants were keen to know what caused their TIDM, and they all wanted to know a lot about management and the long-term results of uncontrolled TIDM, except one participant who stated that there was no point in knowing about the condition, as it could not be prevented. The locus of control was both internal and external as described in Rotter's scale (1966). The symptoms were not visible but could be perceived, though unnoticeable until the stage of coma. The symptoms were thought to be responsible for the illness. All participants wished to be symptom-free and be able to control TIDM well. This encouraged them to seek information about the condition and its management. They stated that they used media and information technology, read books/pamphlets on diabetes, and asked health professionals questions when time permitted.

4.5.2 Strategies to control symptoms

Some participants were upset because TIDM, being omnipresent, restricted them from various activities and foods. For others, there were no problems as long as the condition was under control. The balance between disclosing and concealing was maintained as long as TIDM was well controlled. It seemed difficult for some individuals to maintain good diabetes control and still live a normal life as cited by Goffman (1986). These stigmatised individuals wished to pass for normal.

A couple of participants showed despair. To them, TIDM seemed a horrible condition that was difficult to control because it presents two opposite possible emergencies leading to coma, that is severe hyperglycaemia resulting in excess in diabetic ketoacidosis, and hypoglycaemia, which is a side effect of excess insulin as stated by Williams and Pickup (1999). Inhibition of the condition was possible if the individual was vigilant and followed the regimen to prevent both these acute serious conditions.

4.5.3 Self-identity change

Most participants stated that TIDM had made an impact on their lives as they needed to adjust to it, manage it, and control it. One participant felt let down by his body and was angry that he had it. As cited by Bury (1982), there was some experience of body change. Some participants demonstrated low self-esteem and mentioned that they had lost friends. One of them did not get a job because it was known that he was living with diabetes. Individuals were forced to continuously evaluate themselves against their peers without TIDM while assimilating the condition.

4.5.4 Invalidation/lack of belief

TIDM has no visible physical symptoms to convince the public that the individual is ill until the condition is really out of control or until one becomes unconscious as observed by Cohen and Lazarus (1983) in one of the five modes of coping and adaptation in health and illness. No one believed the diabetic individual to be living with a chronic condition; therefore, the public offered no support or sympathy.

At times even the medical professionals blamed the individual for not controlling the illness as he or she had been told to do. Some members of society lacked understanding and knowledge of diabetes and therefore failed to be of any assistance during an emergency. Others were of the opinion that TIDM resulted from punishment for a wrong deed committed by either the individual concerned or his or her parents.

4.5.5 Social unacceptability of TIDM

The perceived stigma made some participants conceal the condition and maintain privacy during blood glucose checks and the giving of insulin injections. They felt embarrassed and worse in a state of hypoglycaemia, which can lead to being discriminated against by peers, teachers, employers, or any member of the society because of their deviant behaviour (Parsons, 1951). The participants viewed the chronicity of TIDM as a cause of some distress because it did not resolve like acute illness, but they agreed that social support can reduce some stress and the impact on their social lives as noted by Cohen and Lazarus (1983).

4.5.6 Strategies of appearing normal

Participants stated that by controlling TIDM, they were striving to appear normal as if they had no chronic condition. They did not wish to be excluded by society or prevented from doing any activities or holding any jobs. Disclosure was chosen so that the individuals could get sympathy and help from the public in times of need. The minority who did not disclose TIDM was not sure of what would happen to them in case of hypoglycaemia. All participants were aware that disclosure was voluntary. It was easy when the condition was well controlled for the public not to about their condition.

Most participants seemed to be sentimental as if they owned the condition, referring to it as 'my diabetes' as if it were a personal belonging to show that they had adjusted to living with it and were trying to cope

DISCUSSION

with perceived stigma. Balance between disclosing and concealing helped the participants to aim for a normal life (Schneider and Conrad, 1980) as was reported in two forms of disclosure by the individuals with epilepsy to explain their condition and to reduce the stigma.

4.6 Reliability of the instrument

The study explored the experiences of adolescents living with TIDM whilst negotiating/interacting with society. After the selective coding of themes, and after categories emerged from the core categories of assimilation/accommodation and stigmatisation, the following categories were identified as common to most participants whether their responses were positive or negative:

1) Sensemaking, that is, to obtain an understanding and explanation of T1DM. Some participants asked questions such as: 'What caus TIDM?' 'Why do I have to live with TIDM?' 'Is it because I am a naughty child?' 'Were my parents bad?' 'What causes TIDM?' They tried to obtain information about TIDM from all available sources, both human and material.
2) Strategies to manage symptoms, which include an individual's inability to control symptoms of the condition. Individuals worried when they could not control diabetes in spite of giving themselves insulin advised and eating a healthy diet or even engaging in regular physical activity. The symptoms were either those of high blood glucose or low blood glucose. They tried hard to use strategies of control as advised by the medical professionals.
3) Self-identity change, meaning how the individual perceives herself a how adjustments could be made. Some individuals

showed low self-esteem and blamed themselves for failure to manage and cope with diabetes.

4) Invalidation, caused by the invisibility of TIDM, led the public n to believe that the individual had a chronic illness, and thus no sympathy was shown. Society tended not to believe the individuals living wi TIDM or take them seriously.

5) Social unacceptability in life-threatening situations such as diabetic ketoacidosis and hypoglycaemia. This can be used as a strategy f coping with perceived stigma and also to gain sympathy from t society.

6) Strategies to appear 'normal', meaning striving to control TIDM and n to disclose any information about the condition. The individual strives for good control of TIDM so as to pass for normal.

The emerging of the foregoing themes and categories proved that the instrument was reliable because it explored the experiences of adolescents living with TIDM while negotiating with society. It noted the changes in self-identity, adaptation to living with chronic illness and coping with perceived stigma.

5

Conclusion

The study showed that adolescents living with TIDM experience changes in self-identity and perceive stigma whilst interacting with society. This led to their concealing of the condition in order to pass as normal. The health professionals also labelled them as having a physiological disorder with no cure but needed the individual to it. Some participants felt that they had tried on their own to understand TIDM so as to cope with daily living and management of the condition, and others thought the information given by health professionals was adequate. It seemed difficult for some adolescents to live with TIDM and to interact with peers and society in a normal way, especially if their illness was kept private, though there was fear of what could result when an emergency arose. Some adolescents did not know anyone who lived with TIDM, and others had not spoken to anyone who was diagnosed with the same condition. Most participants were striving to appear normal and symptom-free to maintain their own self-identity and self-esteem whilst negotiating with society.

The study has shown that there is a link between body, self, and society (Bury, 2001). Living with TIDM made one too aware of self and how one interacted with society and adapted to living with TIDM.

The study reported similar findings to previous studies done on experiences and perceived stigma in living with chronic illnesses which have no visible physical symptoms unless in an emergency such as coma/seizures. In the study by Schneider and Conrad (1980), two forms of disclosure were noted to balance between disclosing and concealing the condition in order to minimise social stigma, that is by telling other people so as to get support and sympathy and not telling them until they observe an epileptic seizure. The same would apply to those adolescents who concealed their TIDM when they experience a hypoglycaemic state resulting in confusion or coma, which needs understanding and assistance by society.

Various themes were identified and categorised across the whole range of interviews during qualitative analysis as suggested by Scambler and Hopkins (1990). The core categories, namely assimilation and stigmatisation, were finally identified. Some participants had a positive perception, and others responded negatively to the same question, which proves that there are different ways of coping and adjusting to living with any chronic illness. Revealing or concealing TIDM was another form of coping with perceived stigma. Ordinary people do not inject themselves with insulin before meals.

Briggs, Plant, and Devlin (1977) stated that individuals were labelled and stigmatised as colostomies because of their altered body function, which was not helped by what Kelly (1992) reported, namely that the major body function was altered in individuals living with ileostomies after radical surgery even if it was invisible. These people stated that they were reminded as soon as they went to the toilet or stood in front of a mirror.

Negative responses such as 'Living with diabetes is a nightmare' and 'I can't stand or talk about my diabetes' were noted, but there were positive ones like 'Diabetes has taught me to be well organised, and I am happy every day.' Each participant gave a mixture of negative and

CONCLUSION

positive responses, which proves that individuals view the same issues or situations differently. For example, it is tiresome for some individuals to attend a diabetic clinic on a regular basis, and others enjoy frequent visits a lot. In the study to investigate the prevalence of psychological symptoms in a busy diabetic clinic, conducted by Lloyd, Dyer, and Barnett (2000), participants were asked whether they felt that they would like to receive counselling or psychotherapy to help with their diabetes management, and 25 per cent answered affirmatively. One-third reported that they would be interested in receiving counselling or psychotherapy if it were currently available at the diabetic clinic. Those who showed interest in and need for psychosocial support were significantly more likely to report moderate to severe levels of depression and/or anxiety. The study showed that some adolescents seek information to help them to cope with the experiences and the burden of living with T1DM and just give up. Those who were keen to obtain cognitive, affective, and psychomotor skills wanted to be more efficient in dealing with symptoms, diabetic emergencies, and self-management and control of the condition by taking prescribed medication and undergoing behaviour modification. Stigma was either avoided by staying symptom-free and preventing any acute complication or disclosing the condition to the public in case the participants needed assistance and support as reported in the reviewed literature.

6

Implications of the study

The results of the study implied that identified themes from interviews can help in setting strategies for medical management of a chronic condition in order to help individuals to cope with perceived stigma. Another implication was that health professionals need to pay attention even to slight behavioural changes of adolescents living with TIDM so that they may be referred early for counselling as suggested by some studies on chronic illness and diabetes. Psychosocial intervention could be beneficial at the diagnosis stage and done at regular intervals to ensure continuous adaptation and coping skills to allay fears or worries, as suggested by Fife (1994) and Raguram et al. (1996), that perceived stigma will result in not being well psychologically. Therefore a holistic approach should be adopted in the medical management of chronic conditions. The findings in this may or may not improve the care of adolescents living with TIDM. The public need to be educated so that there is more awareness of the different types of diabetes so as to help adolescents to live with TIDM and to decrease the perceived stigma.

7

Limitations of the study

The time allotted was short to collect and analyse qualitative data, and this was worsened by processes pertaining to things such as ethical issues. The sample size was small to explore the experiences of adolescents living with TIDM and to draw conclusions about perceived stigma whilst they interact with society. Nevertheless, this sample represented the population of adolescents aged between sixteen and nineteen years attending the clinic. The relationship of the researcher to the participants might have influenced the respondents as the researcher worked at the same clinic, and therefore the participants might not have disclosed enough, or else they just stated what they thought would please the researcher and discussed only mild experiences to avoid being labelled any further. As noted by Patton (1980), the researcher's theoretical, cultural, and behavioural assumptions might have had an effect on the interpretation of the findings in this study if there was already a hypothesis to prove before undertaking the study.

8

Recommendations

Further research is recommended on the same topic using a bigger sample of adolescents or young adults over an adequate period of time. Triangulation is to be used, that is comparing qualitative and quantitative data in order to ensure reliability and validity (Kirk and Miller, 1986). Holistic approach medicine, that is treating the individual physically, psychologically/emotionally, and socially should be considered as suggested by Armstrong (1986) because of self and identity problems during this stage. Gerhard (1989) confirmed that health professionals need to understand psychology so as to help individuals living with chronic illness deal with overt societal reaction/stigma.

Counselling and psychotherapy should be available and offered to all adolescents living with TIDM so that they can have the choice to attend before any obvious psychological symptoms develop. Ridgeway and Matthews (1982) were of the opinion that psychological preparation was not the only important issue that should be considered, but rather an instruction in methods of cognitively coping with fears and worries needs to be addressed. The advice to individuals living with TIDM tends to focus on the daily management of diabetes and not on how to deal with psychosocial issues until the individual presents psychological symptoms of not coping with the condition due to various reasons.

9

References

Abram, H. S. (1980). 'The Psychology of Chronic Illness'. *Annals, American Academy of Political and Social Sciences* 447: 5–11.

Armstrong, D. (1986). 'The Problem of the Whole Person on Holistic Medicine'. 1: 27–36.

Briggs, M., Plant, J., and Devlin, H. (1997). 'Labelling the Stigmatised: The Carer of the Colostomist'. *Annals of the Royal College of Surgery of England* 59: 247–50.

Bury, M. (1982). 'Chronic Illness as Biographical Disruption'. *Sociology of Health and Illness* 4: 167–82.

Bury, M. (1986). 'Social Constructionism and the Development of Medical Sociology'. *Sociology of Health and Illness* 8: 137–69.

Bury, M. (2001). 'Illness Narratives: Fact or Fiction?' *Sociology of Health and Illness* 23, 3: 236–86.

Carson, C. (2001). 'Risk-Taking Behaviour in the Teenager with Diabetes: The Norm, Not the Exception'. *Diabetes Management* 2, 2: 2–4.

Charmaz, K. (1983). 'Loss of Self: A Fundamental Form of Suffering in the Chronically Ill'. *Sociology of Health and Illness* 5: 168–95.

Charmaz, K. (1987). 'Struggling for Self-Identity Levels of the Chronically Ill'. *Sociology of Health Care* 6: 283–321.

Charmaz, K. (1990). 'Discovering Chronic Illness; Using Grounded Theory'. *Social Science Medicine* 30, 11: 1161–72.
Charmaz, K. (1995). 'Grounded Theory', in N. M. Denzin and Y. S. Lincoln, *Handbook of Qualitative Research*. 2nd edn, London: Sage, 2000.
Cohen, F., and Lazarus, R. S. (1983). 'Coping and Adaptation in Health and Illness', in D. Mechanic (ed), *Handbook of Health, Healthcare, and the Health Professionals*. New York: Free Press.
Conrad, P. (1987). 'The Experience of Illness: Recent and New Directions'. *Research in the Sociology of Health Care* 6: 1–31.
Dancey, C. P., and Backhouse, S. (1997). *IBS: A Complete Guide to Relief from Irritable Bowel Syndrome*. Constable & Robinson.
Donoghue, P. J., and Seigel, M. E. (2000). *Sick and Tired of Feeling Sick and Tired: Living with Invisible Chronic Illness*. 2nd edn, New York: W. W. Norton & Company.
Faro, B. (1999). 'The Effects of Diabetes on Adolescents' Quality of Life'. *Paediatric Nursing* 25, 3: 247–53.
Fife, B. L. (1994). 'The Conceptualization of Meaning in Illness'. *Social Science and Medicine* 38: 309–14.
Gerhardt, N. (1989). *Ideas about Illness: An Intellectual and Political History of Medical Sociology*. London: MacMillan.
Gillham, B. (2000). 'Developing Questionnaire London: Continuum', in N. M. Denzin and Y. S. Lincoln (eds), *Handbook of Qualitative Research*. London: Sage, 2000.
Goffman, E. (1963). *Stigma: Notes on the Management of Spoiled Identity*. Englewood Cliffs, NJ: Prentice Hall.
Goffman, E. (1986). *Stigma: Notes on the Management of Spoiled Identity*. Englewood Cliffs, NJ: Prentice Hall.
Grey, M., Boland, E. A., Sullivan-Bolyai, S., and Tamborlane, W. V. (1998). 'Personal and Family Factors Associated with Quality of Life in Adolescents with Diabetes'. *Diabetes Care* 2: 805–8.

REFERENCES

Idler E. (1979). 'Definitions of Health and Illness and Medical Sociology'. *Social Science and Medicine* 13A: 723–31.

Ing, R., Darko, D., and Hillson, R. M. (2002). 'Street Drug Use among Young Patients with Type 1 Diabetes Mellitus' (unpublished). London: Diabetic Area, Hillingdon Hospital.

Ingersoll, G. M. (1989). *Adolescence.* 2nd edn, Englewood Cliffs, NJ: Prentice-Hall.

Kelly, M. (1991). 'Coping with and Ileostomy'. *Social Science and Medicine* 33: 115–25.

Kelly, M. (1992). 'Self, Identity, and Radical Surgery'. *Sociology of Health and Illness* 14, 3: 391–415.

Kelly, M. P., and Field, D. (1996). 'Medical Sociology of Chronic Illness and the Body'. *Sociology of Health and illness* 18, 2: 241–57.

Kirk, J., and Miller, M. (1986). *Reliability and Validity in Qualitative Research.* London: Sage.

Kleinman, A. (1988). *The Illness Narratives: Suffering, Healing, and the Human Condition.* New York: Basic Books.

Lawrence, C. (1994). *Medicine in the Making of Britain.* London: Routledge.

Lloyd, C. E, Dyer, P. H., and Barnett, A. H. (2000). 'Prevalence of Symptoms of Depression and Anxiety in a Diabetes Clinic Population'. *Diabetic Medicine* 17: 198–205.

Parson, T. (1951). *The Social System.* England: KRP 437.

Patton, M. Q. (1980). *Qualitative Evaluation Methods.* Beverly Hills, CA: Sage.

Pless, I. V., and Roghmann, K. J. (1971). 'Chronic Illness and Its Consequences: Observation Based on Three Epidemiologic Surveys'. *The Journal of Paediatrics* 79, 3: 351–9.

Radley, A. (1997). 'What Does the Body Have in Illness?' in L. Yardley (ed), *Material Discoveries of Health and Illness.* London: Routledge.

Raguram, R., Weiss, M. G., Channabasavanna, S. M., and Devine, G. M. (1996). 'Stigma, Depression, and Somatisation in South India'. *American Journal of Psychiatry* 153: 1043–9.

Ridgeways, V., and Matthews, A. (1982). 'Psychological Preparation for Surgery'. *British Journal of Clinical Psychology* 21: 271–80.

Rotter, J. B. (1966). 'Generalized Expectancies for Internal versus External Control of Reinforcement'. *Psychological Monographs* 80: 1–28.

Scambler, G. (1984). 'Perceiving and Coping with Stigmatising Illness', in R. Fitzpatrick, J. Hinton, G. Scambler, and J. Thompson, *The Experience of Illness*. London: Tavistock.

Scambler, G., and Hopkins, A. (1986). 'Being Epileptic: Coming to Terms with Stigma'. *Sociology of Health and Illness* 8: 26–43.

Scambler, G., and Hopkins, A. (1990). 'Generating a Model of Epileptic Stigma: The Role of Qualitative Analysis'. *Social Science and Medicine* 30, 11: 1187–95.

Schneider, J. W., and Conrad, P. (1980). 'In the Closet with Illness: Epilepsy, Stigma Potential, and Information Control'. *Social Problems* 28, 1: 32–44.

Silverman, D. (1999). *Interpreting Qualitative Data Methods for Analysing Talk, Text, and Interaction*. 2nd edn, London: Sage.

Strauss, A. (1975). *Chronic Illness and the Quality of Life*. St Louis, MO: Mosby.

Strauss, A., and Corbin, J. (1990). *Basics of Qualitative Research: Grounded Theory Procedures and Techniques*. London: Sage.

Williams, G., and Pickup, J. C. (1999). *Handbook of Diabetes*. 2nd edn, London: Blackwell Science.

About the Book

This qualitative study aims to explore the experiences of adolescents living with type 1 diabetes mellitus (TIDM). This is a chronic condition characterised by abnormally high blood glucose brought on by lack of insulin, and it is treated with insulin injections as there is no medical cure. More specifically, the study examines how the sufferer manages the illness and copes with the perception of stigmatisation which is related to this condition. Despite the existence of research into living and coping with some chronic conditions, research on TIDM, particularly with the use of qualitative methodologies, is limited. A review of the literature indicates that research on the stigma associated with chronic illnesses, particularly those which are functional and invisible (i.e. in which the symptoms are not externally visible), is insufficient.

www.ingramcontent.com/pod-product-compliance
Lightning Source LLC
Chambersburg PA
CBHW021431070526
44577CB00001B/159